With A Heart of Thanksgiving

I dedicate this book to my mother, Mandy Coleman Hall. You taught me to follow my heart and to always march to the beat of my own drum. Your strength and tenacity to overcome life's obstacles with grace, dignity, and beauty is what inspires me daily to believe that I can do anything! You are my rock. I love you, Mom. To my father Clarence Hall, Sr. Thank you for mending the fences of my childhood and building a new level of love, understanding, and wisdom in our relationship before you departed from this earth. I love and miss you every day. To my wonderful siblings: Clarence, Walter, Frederick, Jaleesa, Abigail, and Michelle. You all are a continued source of love and support in my life. Thanks for being you. To the Coleman/Hall families, thanks for teaching me the importance of legacy. None of this would be possible without your guidance, care, and belief in me. I love and appreciate all of you. To my inner circle and dearest friends, Katrina Lee and Victor Raphael Robinson- Yarber, thanks for all of your encouragement, fortitude, wisdom, and diligence. Your presence has been priceless throughout this process. Love you to the moon and beyond the stars.

This book is my love letter to every single one of you who desires to become the woman that you were destined by God to be for your future husband, family, community and the world. Always remember to enjoy the journey!

WHILE YOU ARE WAITING

FATIMA L. HALL

While You Are Waiting by Fatima L. Hall
Published by G2 Publishing, Inc.

75 Washington Street, Suite 876, Fairburn, GA 30213
www.fatimalhall.com

Unless otherwise noted, all Scripture quotations are from the Holy Bible, New International Version. Copyright © 1973, 1978, 1984, International Bible Society. Used by permission. Scripture quotations marked KJV are from the King James Version of the Bible.

Book Design:
Jadarien Sanders for J. Designs
info@jdesignsonline.com

Cover Design:
Kevin Tracey for Kevin Mark Photography
kevinmark.pd@gmail.com

Photography:
Tory Brown for Elite Media Studios
info@elitemedia.studio

Make Up Artist:
Robert Maddox for Blakemore Inc.
Blakemoreinc@gmail.com

Hair Stylist:
Demetria Davis
Successstudio06@icloud.com

CONTENT

Before I formed you in the womb I knew you, before you were born I set you apart; I appointed you as a prophet to the nations.

Jeremiah 1:5

PREFACE

When I began writing this book, I knew I would have to come from a very vulnerable space in my life; that I would have to dig deep and touch on some memories and experiences that would stir up a plethora of emotions that I had buried deep. I knew I would have to expose my mistakes, failures, and pain as it relates to love and relationships. But I decided from the first typed word, that if what I have been through could bring change to another woman's life, then it was well worth every tear I would cry and every unsolicited emotion I would feel as I revealed my heart through my fingertips. If you are reading this book, I am pouring out my heart to you. I am exposing my scars so that you may be healed; that you may live a full, happy life with nothing missing and nothing broken.

Everything that you go through prepares you for what you asked God for. I will also go further and declare that everything you go through is not for you, but for someone that you are responsible for helping along life's journey. So let's begin to explore this place that we call waiting. Let's talk about singleness; the proverbial helicopter that just seems to hover in our lives as we try to make sense of all that is happening around us. The place where we go to bed at night with our pillows wet with tears because we are trying not to break under the pressure of what God promised us and the reality of what has yet to manifest. Let's go there so we can find the strength to keep going even when it looks like your life is standing still.

For I know the plans I have for you, declares the LORD, plans to prosper you and not to harm you, plans to give you hope and a future and an expected end.

Jeremiah 29:11

MY STORY

From an early age, my outlook on love was skewed. The first man I ever loved, besides my father, was a male cousin who took me under his wing and affectionately called me Mikey. Some of you may remember the little boy from the Life Cereal commercial who never had an opinion and just accepted whatever the other kids gave him. Well, just like Mikey, he kept me around as a sidekick because I agreed with everything and said nothing. I didn't have an opinion. He said move, I moved. He said get up, I got up. He chose what we ate and I ate it; just like Mikey. I would do anything to stay in his good graces because I didn't want to be rejected. I was quiet and introverted as a child. So, to have someone who was considered cool pay attention to me, to want me around was a feeling that I would give anything not to lose.

Needless to say, experiencing this type of relationship with the opposite sex during my formative years laid the foundation for how I would govern my future relationships with men. I would strive for perfection in my relationships; never wanting to upset my partner and always putting his needs first. But despite all my efforts to be the perfect mate, every man I loved, I lost. Or I would be on cloud nine, floating through my days, enjoying the budding relationship, soaking in the promises of forever and I love yous only to discover, much to my surprise, that in the end he had chosen to commit to someone else.

After experiencing this pattern several times, I became harsh and abrasive. I allowed myself to get totally immersed in my work. I put on my Nike pumps and ran as fast as I could from relationships. Until the day I ran out of myself and into the arms of the Father. I felt tired, broken, and abandoned from the hurts of my past. As I surrendered my will to His, He began to show me why this cycle kept occurring in my relationships. I discovered that I was giving too much too soon to people who did not have the right to occupy that kind of intimate space in my life. I came to grips with the fact that I was the one doing the choosing in my relationships, not God. Instead of opening myself up to allow God to send the right person into my life, I would turn a blind eye to healthy relationships because the person did not look like the "model mate" that I had created in my head.

I came to the harsh reality that I needed to get back on the potter's wheel because I was broken. I had to admit to myself that Perfect Patty was flawed. I had the wrong outlook on love and relationships and I was going to have to allow God to undo everything I had learned and experienced throughout the course of my life. I would have to wait; not idle or in a complacent state, but with expectancy. I was perplexed. How could this be? Why do I have to wait? I have friends and people around me who don't have themselves together but they are already married. Why me? God's answer was simple, why not you?

My sisters, as we embark upon this spiritual journey to wholeness, fulfillment, and happiness together, it is my desire that you discover two very important things: that you matter and you are worth the wait. No matter what anyone else has told you. No matter how they tried to break your spirit. Remember, the more pressure applied, the more precious the diamond becomes.

Wisdom is of utmost importance, therefore get wisdom, and with all your effort work to acquire understanding.

Proverbs 4:7

1

Singleness Is Not A Curse, It's A Course

Singleness will cause you to feel like the odd man out. As you watch your friends marry and have children, you begin to question if God has forgotten about you. You ask yourself, "Has He heard my prayers? Is there something wrong with me? Why does the relationship cycle of life keep passing me by?" God has not forgotten about you. He is very much aware of what you need and even what you want. But what we have to learn to do is trust His timing. Most importantly, we have to utilize the time He has given us before marriage wisely and resist the temptation to adopt the mindset that life begins once you say, "I do". In fact, it is quite the contrary. Life begins the day you say, "I will". I will what you may ask? The answer is simple, embrace your destiny and walk in it. Before you can think of committing to someone else, the first commitment you must make is to yourself. Life begins with a personal commitment to fulfill the destiny that you were created for. Sounds a little selfish, doesn't it? Actually, it's a very necessary part of life that we as women have not been taught to embrace. When you commit to other things and other people before you commit to yourself, you become empty and ultimately unfulfilled. Singleness is the time to make a commitment to yourself so that when your husband does come into your life, he is attracted to the fulfillment, happiness, and peace that you have already created for yourself. His presence should add to that, not be the source of it.

Everyone's path is different. No two stories are ever the same. Although we may have similarities in our paths, God has uniquely designed yours just for you. So resist the urge to compare yourself and God's timing in your life to that of others. Most importantly, stop allowing your progress to be ruled by time. There are goals in life that will seem impossible to achieve. At times, people will give up on you and even count you out. They will never expect you to have what God says you will have because they are judging you based on the world's concept of time. They will be more concerned about your biological clock than you are; and count down the days, hours, and minutes for you. Do not lose heart. Do not lose focus. Stay in the game and keep your eyes on the prize. Everything you desire, according to His will for your life, God will manifest. Trust God at His Word. If He says He is going to do it, He will do exactly what He said.

I discovered in my own life that if God had already fulfilled His promise of marriage and children, this book would have never been written. The blessing that God has for someone through this manuscript would not exist. God will hold back His promises in our lives to bring us to the realization that our first commitment is to the work that He wants to accomplish through us. To reveal to us that we are part of something greater than what we want or desire for ourselves.

So what is it that you have not accomplished because you are fixated on a promise that has not manifested? Could it be that while you are waiting on God to give you what you want, He is actually waiting on you to align your will with His so He can lead you to it? He is waiting on you to accomplish the things He has placed in you because your obedience is what will get you to the promise.

It is very easy to get sacrifice confused with obedience. I used to say, "God, I have given You my life. I have given You everything I have." His response to me was, "But have you done what I asked you to do? Have you accomplished the things I need you to accomplish on this earth so that I can unlock the door to the things you desire most?" There is a reason for every season. Therefore, as a single woman, you must understand the importance of this season in your life and act on it accordingly. Waiting on God has nothing to do with standing still. It has everything to do with moving forward.

66 *I remain confident of this: I will see the goodness of the LORD in the land of the living.* 99

Psalms 27:13

2

While You Are Waiting, God Is Working: The Helicopter Effect

Evolution by definition is the gradual development of something, especially from a simple to a more complex form. Life is a constant stream of events; ever evolving and ever increasing or decreasing in momentum. To master this journey called life, you must understand that you are not actually waiting for that next career move, or the love of your life, or that beautiful family; you are actually evolving and moving so you will be in position to receive the blessing when it comes. Often times, due to set backs and disappointments along the path of life, we become stagnant and begin to lose hope in the promises that God has made to us. At these moments, man-made time can become our worst enemy because we begin to get anxious, count down the days on the calendar, and even measure our worth as women based on that dreaded biological clock. God did not make time. He allowed the invention of time to manifest on the earth, but He has never and will never govern Himself based on this man-made principle. You must also understand that He is the God of a finished work. Which means the events of your life were already mapped out and written in heaven before you were a twinkle in your father's eye or your mother's pride and joy.

So why worry about the course of a path that has already been mapped out for you? All we have to do is walk in it. God's promises give us hope and direction. If He says you're going to be the mother of beautiful children and you are over 40 years old based on man's standard of time, then expect that you will be a mother of beautiful children in your forties. If God promised that you would have that dream job or business and you are currently struggling to make ends meet, or haven't experienced career advancement in years, believe that He will allow your path to cross with the right person at the right time to make that vision a reality. Your only responsibility is to keep evolving in the right direction until you get there.

Throughout the Bible we see how the "Hall of Famers" were bold enough to take The Creator at His Word by putting their faith into action. Even in the case of Abraham and Sarah, she fell off the path to promise by allowing Hagar to conceive Ishmael with her husband. But God still allowed their promised seed, Isaac, to be born. Abraham still became the father of many nations as God had promised although he nor Sarah were physically able, by man's standards, to bear children. So what is the message here? Even when we try to take matters into our own hands, God still will not allow us to fail. We may create our own setbacks, but failure is never an option when you are walking by faith.

During the evolution process, you must also resist the temptation to compare your life with the people around you. Yes, you should be happy for others and celebrate their victories, but do not let that be the measuring rod for your own personal success. Tell yourself every day that you are evolving, not waiting. Keep God's vision for your life at the forefront of your heart and be mindful of the people who you allow to be around you during this pivotal season. Some people will maintain their presence in your life just to have a front row seat to watch you fail; not to hold you up and cheer you on to the finish line.

To understand how the evolution process works, you must grasp a concept

I like to call the "helicopter effect". What do I mean by this? Well, I'm glad you asked. The unique thing about a helicopter is that it is the only aircraft that can hover in the same spot and still be moving at the same time. You see, although it may seem like the helicopter is not moving, all of its functions are still in operation. It may look stagnant but the propellers are still moving and the engine is still running. In fact, when a helicopter hovers, the earth's gravitational pull below it and the air above it work together to move the vessel so it remains consistent with the earth's rotating axis. Therefore, when it is time to descend, no matter how long the aircraft has been hovering, it will land at the same location that it took off from. In other words, it will land exactly where it is supposed to be.

I'm sure you are thinking, ok now how does this apply to my life as a single woman? Well again, I'm glad you asked. Faith, like the air above the helicopter, is constantly propelling you towards your promise. And just like the earth's gravitational pull below the helicopter, God's timing is shifting things in the atmosphere on your behalf. Although it may look like you are standing still, when your faith aligns with God's timing, you will land at your exact place of destiny. Yes my sister, you will be exactly where you are supposed to be. So remember to inhale the positive and exhale the negative. Keep evolving, keep growing, and most importantly, keep going. Because while you are waiting, God is working!

66 *Trust in and rely confidently on the LORD with all your heart and do not rely on your own insight or understanding. In all your ways know and acknowledge and recognize Him, and He will make your paths straight and smooth [removing obstacles that block your way].* **99**

Proverbs 3:5-7

3

Marrying For Where You Are vs. Marrying For Where You Are Going

Often times in relationships, we marry for where we are, not for where we're going. It's an honest course of action because we meet someone, fall in love, and those around us celebrate and approve of the relationship. People say things like, "You two look good together. You are going to make some beautiful babies". So, ultimately we take the next logical step which is marriage. The honeymoon period is over and the reality that you will be spending the rest of your life with this person sets in. Life goes on, children are born, and careers are established. Then one day, the soul searching begins. Your dreams awaken the drive in you and you begin to feel this burning desire for something more out of life. You realize that there is a thirst in your soul that is still unquenched. Excited about your discovery, you candidly share this with your spouse. But they are neither excited nor supportive. "We have bills to pay and children to raise. There is no time for dreaming," they say. So you tuck your aspirations away quietly and settle into the gig. All the while, resentment creeps in quietly until the elephant becomes so big in the room, you find yourselves living separate lives.

This is what happens when we choose our mate based on the tangible and not the intangible qualities in a person. Intangible or aesthetic qualities in a person appeal to the eye and are volatile while intangible qualities are those things that appeal to the soul and are constant. So it is more important to marry someone who connects with your soul than someone who looks good to your eye. It's like a beautifully wrapped box. It is appealing to the eye and you want to open it, but you won't know if anything is actually in it until you shake it up a bit.

Men often marry based on timing and women marry for security. Timing goes something like this. Well, she was there when my mom died and I needed someone to fill that void. Or, she was with me when I didn't have anything. So, it's only right that we get married now that I do. Security sounds like this. He has an excellent job with benefits. So, I can raise the children and won't have to worry about the finances. Or, he has his own house and a nice car. So I will be well taken care of. But how are any of these tangible qualities, despite how wonderful they sound, tied to your destiny? Just because a person fits your needs at 25, it doesn't mean they will have the capacity to cover the person you will evolve into at 35. If you do not know what your destiny is, do yourself and the other person a favor and don't get married until you do. If you do know what your calling is, then make sure you choose a mate that's going in the same direction; someone who has the capacity to hold your future, not just your attention.

God knows your end from your beginning. He created you before the foundation of the earth. So, He knows where you will be months, days, years, even decades from now. He has designed a mate just for you. But are you willing to wait? Again, I'm not referring to physically standing still or remaining stagnant. What I am asking is, are you willing to allow God to form you in His image?

Many of us are underdeveloped when we say "I do". Just like a cake taken from the oven too soon, we're golden brown on the outside but full of dough and undone on the inside. A soul mate is developed from the inside out. They don't just look good to the eye, they possess the intangible qualities that are good for the soul. A soul mate is not just someone who fits you, they are a reflection of you. When you look into their eyes you should see yourself. When you look into their soul, you should see your destiny. However, many of us marry the one who looks complete on the outside without allowing time to reveal if they are fully developed on the inside.

While in the grocery store, I decided to purchase one of those individual microwave cakes. I had a taste for cake, but didn't want to go through the process of baking one from scratch. It looked good on the box, the directions were simple enough, plus it was on sale. So I thought to myself, this should satisfy my craving and I don't have to spend time slaving over a recipe. When I got home, I followed the quick, simple instructions, popped the batter in the microwave and set it for the specified time. When I opened the microwave, it looked perfect; all nice and golden brown. So, I let it cool, slathered it with frosting and commenced to enjoy my "quick fix". Much to my surprise, when I cut the cake and took a bite it was spongy and doughy on the inside. Not what I imagined at all. I was disappointed and upset with myself at the same time. Because I knew if I had gone through the process of baking the cake instead of trying to replace it with a quick fix, I would be enjoying a decadent piece of cake right now. I would have created something I could be proud of and even share with others. Like that cake, we live in a microwave society where you can have and do everything fast. This mentality is a detriment to the relationship process because everything you need to know about the man you are dating will reveal itself in time.

So, what do you do while you are waiting? The answer is simple, keep moving. Get in the presence of God and ask Him to mold you, shape you, and "bake" you into the woman He would have you to be. It doesn't mean that you will be perfect. Yes, you may still have some lumps in your personality or you may still be a little rough around the edges. Truth be told, some of my best tasting cakes were a little lopsided. But there's nothing that a little extra frosting can't fix. Your imperfections are just right for the man that God has for you. But don't be in such a rush to get married that you choose a mate who is undone; or even worse, he finds you incomplete. Ask God for clarity on your career path, your goals, and your aspirations. Make sure they are clear to you before you try to articulate them to a potential mate.

Ladies, it may require that we limit those phone conversations or take a break from social media to meditate on the Word and simply listen for God's voice. Yes, you read it right. You will need to spend some time alone before you will be ready for your mate. During that time get in the Word, fast, pray, keep a journal, and most importantly, listen. Listen for God's voice as if your life depends on it because ultimately it does.

Taking this time could mean the difference between you discovering your soul mate or just choosing a mate. It could mean the difference between a balanced, healthy, happy partnership and settling for a mediocre marriage. Yes, it's just that serious folks! Remember, before Jesus made any monumental moves on this earth, he spent time consecrated in the presence of God. Away from the distractions of his disciples (friends) and Mary and Joseph (family). You will need to do the same. No, I am not telling you to be super spooky and cut yourself off from the world. Your husband is not going to find you in your prayer closet. But I am encouraging you to get in His presence and let Him lead you to a mate who understands, covers, and supports your divine purpose.

" *Neither do people pour new wine into old wineskins. If they do, the skins will burst; the wine will run out and the wineskins will be ruined. No, they pour new wine into new wineskins, and both are preserved.* "

Matthew 9:17

4

All My Single Ladies

This chapter is probably the nearest and dearest to my heart because this is real life for me. I am a single, successful woman. I make my own money. I have my own things. But I am still without a companion at 40 plus years old. From the outside, life looks great. I travel, spend quality time with my friends and family, and enjoy the simple pleasures of life. But every day I wake up with a void that I pray continuously for God to fill with a companion and children. I wonder, will this ever happen for me? Have I done something to make God turn his face from me in this area of my life?

Some days I feel lost, abandoned, and even angry. How could I serve God with all my heart and He never gives me the desires of my heart? Is this possible? Could God really hate me that much? If so, what did I do to deserve His wrath? Does this scenario sound familiar? Can you relate to my personal testimony?

Truth is, I don't have answers to these questions. But what I do have is His promises that I hold close to my heart. It's what helps me tie a knot at the end of the rope and hang on when I feel like letting go. I know that He's building my faith. I know that when my back is up against the wall, His promises help me to keep my eyes on Him.

Just like a grape is pressed to reveal its sweetness and its essence is then placed in a bottle until it is aged to perfection, God does the same with us as single women. Instead of viewing yourself as too old or past your prime, see yourself the way God sees you; as His fine wine being perfected for the right connoisseur with the perfect pallet. The use of wine in communion is symbolic not only because it represents the blood of Christ, but it also represents the evolution process to fulfilling His purpose on the cross. The one act of obedience that would define His destiny for all eternity.

God has a plan uniquely designed for you. Be bold enough to believe that it will happen; yet patient enough to allow it to manifest at the right time and in the right season. The key to waiting is not waiting at all. It is evolving until you get there. It is your attitude while embracing the evolution process that unlocks the door to your destiny. What you make happen for others, God will make happen for you and so much more. When you serve with a glad heart, He will give you the desires of your heart. Do your part by accomplishing the goals that God has set for you and watch Him open the door for your dreams to become your reality. Know that God is for you, never against you. He keeps His promises. There is no lack, failure, or disappointment when we follow His perfect plan. If you dare to trust Him, He will exceed your expectations and supersede your wildest dreams.

So give yourself a break! Resist the temptation of allowing the world to label you or diminish your worth because you are a single woman of a certain age. Your singleness does not define you. It is the fulfillment of your purpose that does. You are chosen, you are precious to the Father, and you are priceless. Know that you are being preserved for the perfect wine connoisseur who will appreciate your age, texture, and taste. Allow your spirit to be renewed today. Be confident in your path. Your journey isn't over. A new phase is just beginning.

" We can rejoice, too, when we run into problems and trials, for we know that they help us develop endurance. "

Romans 5:3

5

When The Ones Closest To You, Fail You

I remember a particular incident that happened when I was in high school. During that time, I was known as one of the "cool kids" and was dating one of the captains of the varsity basketball team. He was the star athlete and I was the head cheerleader; a match made in high school heaven. It gets no better than that, right? Well, needless to say, every year my mother would ship us off to Orlando for spring break. This particular year, I wasn't feeling it. I really wanted to stay at home and chill with my boyfriend and friends. But, I reluctantly made the trip anyway and subsequently had a great time. I talked to my boyfriend a few times while I was in Orlando and I wasn't able to detect that anything was different. Oh, but it was. When I returned to school that Monday, my friends were acting a little strange. It was as if everybody knew something that I didn't. But, I kept going through the day, excited to have lunch with my boyfriend as I usually did. When I arrived at our spot, I turned the corner anticipating seeing his gorgeous smile. There he was in the midst of his basketball buddies, lips locked with one of my best friends who was also on the cheerleading squad. My heart sank, my body went numb, and I quickly walked out of the room before anyone saw me. I was devastated. How could this be happening to me? When did this happen and why didn't anyone have the decency to tell me?

My disappointment quickly turned to frustration, which then turned to anger in a matter of minutes. I stormed into the room, walked over to him and grabbed him by the collar. I was so blacked out with anger, before I knew it, I was screaming to the top of my lungs and hitting him with the little strength I had left. The young lady, who was supposed to be my friend, left the scene immediately; running like a vicious dog was nipping at her heels. I was so enraged, that I had created the perfect storm of emotions. Once a couple of his friends pulled me off of him, he asked if we could talk.

I was breathing as hard as a pit-bull in a dog fight by then, but I managed to say ok. We left the room and found a quiet hallway and the conversation escalated to argument status quickly. I realized that all of my good deeds, looks, and popularity were no match for what my friend was giving him. But I was determined to stay committed to the promise I made to God to stay a virgin throughout high school. I felt like my world was crashing around me. How was I going to save face and move past this? Where was the script to help me navigate through this tragedy and find poetic justice? Who was going to come to my rescue and tell me it will be alright as I had done for countless others? At that moment, the most popular girl in the school found herself alone, hurt, and embarrassed.

I would find myself here countless times until I learned a very simple truth. People will disappoint you. When they do, just know that they are playing their role in building your story. Another important key to the evolution process is learning how to navigate through life's hurts and disappointments without allowing them to break you. Pain serves a purpose. So what if he married her and not you. Or if she got the promotion and you didn't. Keep evolving. Yes, your father may not have been there or your mother may not have ever supported you. Use that as fuel to drive you forward to your destiny.

Every hurt you have experienced is uniquely designed to shape you into the person that you are supposed to be. You will never be able to truly appreciate a win, if you have never experienced the pain of losing.

As my good friend Kirk Franklin said, pain is necessary. Because it is the pains of life that prepare you for greatness. Anything that becomes a masterpiece goes through a painful process. A piece of marble must be chiseled to become a priceless statue. A diamond must be cut several times before it becomes a precious stone. So it is with our lives. It is the pain that shapes you, molds you, and prepares you for the Master's use. It is your pain that breathes life into your purpose. You see, if I had never been cut by life experiences, I would have never been able to write this book. I would not be able to reveal my scars so that others can be healed. Oftentimes we run from the people who hurt us when they were actually sent by God to prepare us. To truly know what you need and want in a spouse, you must first experience what you don't. So yes, you had to go through that bad break up or that bitter divorce. The pain was necessary. It did not come to kill you, it came to make you stronger and wiser!

Some hurts God will allow to keep happening until we learn to change our habits. When I was young, I valued performance over substance. I learned throughout the course of life that I had to allow patience and time to reveal a person's character. When someone shows you who they are, believe them the first time and remove yourself from the situation. If they choose to change, then watch their evolution process from a distance. Every situation does not require participation; no matter how much you love them. The very area where you are called to make the biggest impact is the place where you will experience the most hurt. Don't run from it. Embrace it as part of your journey.

People will study your life, watch for those uncovered moments, and formulate a strategy to steal that relationship, job, or position right from under you. Here's your measuring rod. If they were able to take it from you, then it wasn't God's best for you. Stop holding on to the former things that brought you pain and open your heart and hands to the greater blessings that God has in store for you. Break the cycle. Do not allow your evolution process to be hindered because you are giving time and attention to the wrong things and people. Resist the temptation to hover over the wrong things when you have every opportunity to gravitate towards the right things. My sister, what is for you, is for you. I'm not saying that you will not be void of struggles or that you may not have to fight for your destiny. If that were the case, then there would be no need for spiritual warfare or for us to put on the whole armor of God daily. But what I am saying is if what you are fighting for takes more away from you, than it adds to you, do yourself a favor and let it go.

❝❝ *Now faith is confidence in what we hope for and assurance about what we don't see.* ❞❞

Hebrews 11:1

6

Fear vs. Faith

I had an interesting conversation with a friend of mine recently. Some of the things she said stuck with me and I continued to ponder them as I laid down to rest. It's amazing how we allow fear of the unknown to talk us out of our greatest blessings. Faith cannot abide where fear exists. Fear speaks loud, but says nothing. It shows up like a thick haze of smoke with the sole intent of clouding our judgment and deterring us from walking into the greatest moments of our lives. Fear by definition is an unpleasant emotion caused by the belief that someone or something is dangerous, likely to cause pain, or a threat. Adversely, faith in its purest form is the depth and breadth of all that we hope for. It is the evidence of those things that we can't see. There is no fear in God's plan for our lives. To activate His promises, we must apply faith. The Word of God is full of faith walkers who did not allow their age, social status, or position in life to stop them from achieving His best. The Lord told Abraham and Sarah that they would give birth to a promised child well past their child bearing years. And they did. After Ruth lost everything, God restored her and made her the wife of one of the most prominent men in a region that was foreign to her. Joseph was sold and betrayed by his brothers after sharing his dream that they would bow before him because one day he would be king. And they did.

Fear is the opposite of faith. Fear is crippling and debilitating. It can make you want to give up, run and hide, and refuse to face the very mountain that God wants to move on your behalf. Adversely, faith is liberating. It evokes joy, freedom, and restores your sense of purpose. Faith gives you the strength to keep going when everything around you speaks defeat. Choosing to activate your faith doesn't mean that things will be easy. It doesn't guarantee that you will never face setbacks, troubles, or obstacles. But what it does guarantee is that in the midst of it all, God is with you. And having God with you is more than the world against you!

Fear of the unknown also exists in our relationships. It can choke the life out of a thriving friendship that could ultimately lead down the path to a beautiful courtship. When we fear losing someone, we actually smother the relationship because we don't give it space to grow. For example, you meet someone whom you gel with very well. You spend a healthy amount of time together and the relationship is progressing. Then out of nowhere, fear starts to creep into your mind and it invites its cousin doubt to the party that's going on in your head. You begin to challenge the person's motives towards you or question their every move. Eventually, the relationship takes a downward spiral and you pacify your behavior by saying to yourself, I knew he would leave me. They all do.

But what part did you play in this cycle of defeat? Did you take a look at yourself? Were you honest about the drama queen that fear of losing him brought out in you? Our past experiences can serve as fuel to motivate us or destroy us. Fear is like gas. The same substance that can start an engine, can burn a building to the ground. Fear can be resourceful or destructive depending on how it is used. We miss some of the greatest blessings in life because we are afraid to silence the voice of fear. So what have you allowed fear to talk you out of? A promotion, an amazing relationship, writing that book, or buying that house? My sister, fear and faith are as real as you allow them to be. So activate your faith and allow your fears to fuel your passion.

> *With God on our side we will win; he will defeat our enemies.*

Psalms 108:13

7

Wake Up The Winner In You

Everyone wants to be successful. I mean, who doesn't want financial stability, a beautiful family, and all those other things that come along with what society deems as the "good life". We all want it. There is nothing wrong with wanting a better life. But if that is your goal, then you must start where you are. First, look at those obstacles in your life that may be hindering your forward advancement; things like your credit score, education level, or maybe your current job. What are you doing to better these situations? Are you praying and waiting on God to do it? Or have you set goals and are working towards completing them daily? You want to buy a new home and stop renting. But are you working to resolve the delinquent accounts that are effecting your credit score? You want to move from a job to a career. But have you looked into furthering your education or researched what it takes to reach your career goals?

As believers, we are often crippled by what we hear from the pulpit. I know that sounds blasphemous, but stay with me for a moment. We are taught that God will make a way out of no way; that our blessing is around the corner or on the way. So we sit on that promise when God is waiting for us to get up and get to work. The Bible says faith without works is dead. So, if we are not putting in the work to achieve those things we have faith for, then we are actually working against His will instead of in it. Your works bring life to what you are believing God for. Just as nothing of substance can live in the Dead Sea, your dreams cannot thrive and become reality in a space where there is no faith.

Now for clarity, understand that I am not telling you to run behind every whim or opportunity that comes to you or that someone may tell you is good for you. However, I am encouraging you to start living your life on purpose. A woman who walks in purpose never has to chase people, opportunities, or even a mate. Her light causes people and opportunities to pursue her. You want to win at life? Well winning starts with knowing who you are and that you are enough. When God gave Moses the charge to go before Pharaoh and demand that he free the children of Israel, He didn't give him an army of soldiers to overtake the kingdom, He simply asked what was in his hand. The staff that Moses carried looked simple to some, but was made to be a mighty weapon when used to fulfill his purpose.

For years I lived waiting on God to pour out those blessings that I would not have room enough to receive. But I was stagnant; just living, existing, and making it happen from day to day. On the outside, I looked successful. But inside I knew I wasn't even close to living the life that God had for me. As the years rolled by and frustration began to set in, I looked to the Father for answers. Then the light came on one day and I discovered that the tools I needed to change my life were in my hand. I didn't need more money, I needed to learn how to be a good steward over the provision that God had already given me. If I wanted a bigger home, then I needed to fix my credit. If I wanted to be married, then I needed to go somewhere else besides work, church, and home so I could meet someone. I realized that I had to stop waiting for God to do it and put some work to all this great faith I had. Understand that in order for the blessings of God to overtake you, you must first be moving towards a goal. God is not Publisher's Clearing House. He is not going to show up at your door with an oversized check. Just as He challenged Moses to use what was in his hand, everything that you need to fulfill the destiny that God has for you is in yours. Take back your life, my sister. Stop waiting and start working. Don't sit and wait for what you want to come to you, go get it! That's what winners do.

There is no difficult equation to living on purpose. Think about the thing that you would do for free; the thing that if no one ever paid you for, you would still wake up every morning excited to do it. Or that thing that makes you unique that no one can do quite like you. That is your passion which is ultimately your purpose. Now once you have identified what that thing is, begin to pray for direction. Do the necessary research on how to turn your passion into your purpose. Study people who are already a success at what you want to do. I guarantee that you will discover a pattern that is consistent throughout each story. Take that knowledge, tweak it, and make it your own. Create your plan of action and carry it through. Goals are simply dreams with deadlines. If you get derailed by life, regroup and get back on track. Pursuing your purpose is like riding a bike. You may fall off, but it doesn't mean you forgot how to ride.

66 *Brethren, I count not myself to have apprehended: but this one thing I do, forgetting those things which are behind, and reaching forth unto those things which are before, I press toward the mark for the prize of the high calling of God in Christ Jesus.* **99**

Philippians 3:13-14

8

Are You A Trophy Piece Or A Centerpiece?

I have always found myself in a position with men where they meet me, they are immediately attracted to my outward appearance, and want to invite me to their best friend's cookout or their gig with the band. At first, I'll admit, it was flattering. All of the compliments about being beautiful and so well put together had my ego on ten. As these relationships progressed, I realized that I was ok for the appearances, but these men didn't take me seriously when it came to building a relationship. Eventually, I found out that some of them were married and in other instances they were gay and needed a beard. But in each situation, I realized that I was nothing more than a trophy piece. An ornamental fixture that men pull down off the shelf and dust off when it is time to look good in front of their friends, but put right back on the shelf once show and tell is over. When this pattern finally became clear, I started to get frustrated. Why was I viewed as the trophy piece and not the centerpiece in any of these men's lives?

After intense self-examination and prayer, I realized that these types of superficial relationships are what I had accepted as my standard. It was I who didn't truly believe that I deserved depth or commitment in a relationship. As long as I was "on the scene" or the red carpet, that was good enough for me. But judging from the loneliness I felt when all the fanfare was over, clearly it wasn't. I realized that God had designed me to be more than just a trophy piece. I was designed to be the centerpiece in the right man's life. I realized that relationships for me had become once again about performance instead of substance.

So, now that I have discovered these behaviors and how they were affecting my relationships, what do I need to do to correct them? Well, first I had to become comfortable with a very basic fact. People will treat you the way you allow them to. If you do not set the tone for what you want from a relationship, then don't expect the other party to guess and get it right. You see, many of us are so desperate for companionship that we will accept anything; even if it goes against our better judgment. Although we won't admit it, we adopt the mindset that having a piece of a man is better than having no man at all. So, we allow him to take the lead in the relationship and we fall in line with his expectations. Only to end up in the same place that we started, single and alone.

Have you ever been in a public place and witnessed a child completely show out on the parent? I mean kicking and screaming in the middle of the department store floor because they couldn't get what they wanted. These situations happen because the parent did not take the time behind closed doors to set the level of expectancy for the child's behavior while in public. So, whatever they are allowed to get away with at home is magnified when there is an audience. Men are the same way. When a man acts in a negative way towards you in private that you know is beneath your standards and you give him a pass because you really like him, what your actions are relaying to him is that it's ok to treat you that way. The more you allow these behaviors to persist, the higher on the shelf you go. The more of a play thing you become. And who takes a toy seriously? No one.

Men respect women who articulate their standards. I hear you saying, "But what if I articulate my standards and he leaves me?" Then he is not the man for you. Let him go. The person that God has for you will not only respect your standards, but he will work to meet and exceed them. Now let's talk about how to articulate your standards. Society teaches women through reality television and social media that projecting attitude or speaking loudly is the way to gain respect from men. My sister, those behaviors are not necessary. In fact, you rarely have to be confrontational at all. When your man says or does something that is inappropriate, just take a step back. Begin to scale back on the attention that you are giving him. When he feels you pulling away, he will do everything in his power to get back in your good graces. When he asks you what's wrong or starts to ask questions to get you to talk, that's the window of opportunity to share your feelings and articulate your standards. In public or around friends is not the time to have this type of dialogue. It should be in a private, intimate setting where it's just you and him.

I remember meeting this guy on Tinder. We went out on a few dates and had a nice time. He invited me over for dinner one Sunday afternoon and introduced me to his son. Now anyone who knows me will testify to the fact that I have a soft spot for children. If you want to lure me in, a cute kid is definitely my kryptonite. We continued seeing each other and my relationship with his son developed quickly. So, one evening we're laying on the couch watching television and he says to me, "You want a relationship with me, don't you?" I paused for a moment thinking this is a rather odd question. Then I said, "Well if we have the right chemistry and things continue to progress in that direction, then yes I guess I would." He turned to me and said, "I don't want that kind of relationship. I have no desire to ever get married." At first, I was stunned. But once I digested what he said to me, I got up, grabbed my things, kissed him on the forehead, and left. Needless to say, he called me several times and eventually I answered. We continued to date for a while but the relationship was one of the worst I had ever experienced. In fact, he started to pick and choose the times he wanted to see me and eventually confessed that he was seeing multiple women. Yes, once again I had become a trophy piece and not the centerpiece in yet another man's life. You see, a shelf can hold several trophies, but a table can only have one centerpiece.

After I finally broke off the relationship, I did some soul searching to try to make sense of why I ended up perpetuating the same cycle over and over again. I fasted and prayed and God took me back to what I shared with you all earlier. My outlook on relationships was damaged. From an early age, I learned that if you say nothing and don't articulate your standards, then he will stay. But just like in this case, they never did. And more importantly, I kept wasting something I could never get back, my time. Ladies, I cannot stress this enough. When a man, or anyone for that matter, shows you who they really are, believe them the first time. When I walked out of his house that day, my actions articulated my standards. But I was not spiritually or mentally strong enough to reinforce them with my words. I let loneliness, my age, and the bond that I had formed with his son stop me from standing by a decision that would have ultimately kept me from wasting precious, valuable time.

Here's a scenario to better explain how important it is to value your time. Let's say that in your lifetime you will date ten potential mates before you get to the eleventh one who is destined to be your husband. If you dedicate two to three years of your life trying to cultivate relationships with each of these men even after you know that it's not going anywhere, how much time have you wasted? Listen, if God allowed the children of Israel to wander around for forty years on a journey that should have taken them eleven days, do you honestly think that He won't allow you to do the same? God's plan consists of a series of events, tests, and victories that will ultimately lead you to your promised life. We make the process to the promise longer than it has to be because we gravitate towards relationships that hold us back. We invest our time in people whose sole purpose is to get us off track. It's your choice as to whether your journey takes 4 years or 40. The key is, you must learn to use your time wisely.

When it comes to dating, waiting must become an action word. When you meet a potential mate, ask the hard questions before you allow yourself to become emotionally invested. Don't be afraid to articulate your standards. If he walks away, then guess what, you are one step closer to the man that God has for you. I cannot stress this point enough. You will stay in the same place you are in and continue to repeat the same cycles in relationships if you don't learn how to pass this simple test. Often times the writing is on the wall, but we are just too afraid to read it.

To get to the man that God has for you, you must learn to date with intention. It takes more strength to hold on to something that no longer serves you than it does to let go and trust God. If you are sitting at a table where love is no longer being served and the fulfillment you seek is not being reciprocated, gather your strength and get up. God has a table prepared for you and a harvest of blessings like you have never seen before. You are meant to be a centerpiece my sister, never a trophy piece.

" *Don't be gullible. Check out everything, and keep only what's good. Throw out anything tainted with evil.* **"**

1 Thessalonians 5:21-22

9

When Life Hands You Lemons, Throw Them Back!

Being single doesn't mean that you will be frolicking through the lilies every day, just you and God. There will be times when you will get lonely. There will be times when you want to settle. There are times when your body will start craving the intimacy that you so richly desire. God has a way of taking us through valley experiences so we can appreciate the view from the mountaintop. But my sister, no matter how lonely or frustrated with the process you become, if life hands you a lemon, throw it back.

Lemons are the type of men that are appealing on the outside but completely sour on the inside. They are the ones that will waste your time and have no desire to date you with intention. He is the kind of guy who feeds off of instant gratification but has nothing to offer in the long run. Now how many men in your phone contacts list came to mind as you read this? No need to be embarrassed. I have a few lemons in mine as well.

The hurry up and wait of life will lead you to believe that there is no time to go through a process. Think about it, in the midst of 24 hour stores, online shopping, and lightning fast file transfers, there's hardly anything you can't have fast. So when the culture we live in is challenged by the divine order of God's process, it causes hurry up and wait moments in your life that can be hard to understand. Since God is not governed by time, when we pray for change, He is more concerned about whether or not we are ready for what we've asked for than actually fulfilling our prayer request.

Now let's get back to these lemons, shall we? So how do you know if you're dealing with a lemon? Here are a few traits to look for:

1. He has no short-term or long-term goals: Ladies, if he cannot articulate to you what his goals are six months, one year, or five years from now, throw him back. You are dealing with a lemon. If he does not have a vision for his own life, then there is no way that he can lead a family.

2. He constantly speaks negatively about his mother or children's mother: I would be remiss if I said that I believe every mother is perfect. In fact, there are mothers in this world who hurt, neglect, and abuse their children. It is an awful, gut-wrenching truth. But if you are dealing with a man who still has a chip on his shoulder because of how his mother treated him as a child, then you may want to give it some time before you begin to seriously consider dating him. Also, if a man constantly has negative things to say about the mother of his children, this is a definite sign that he has not matured in his dealings with women. Be very leery of the man who always finds the opportunity to degrade or defame the mother of his children. He is most likely trying to recruit you on his team before you've had the chance to see the whole playbook. I once dated a guy who had so many negative things to say about his child's mother that I started to form an invalid opinion about her. Once I got to know this woman, I found out that she was the driving force behind making sure that he had a presence in his child's life. Not only that, when the child came to stay with his father during his scheduled visitation times, she would send back half or sometimes all of the child support money she received for that month to make sure he could buy food and do activities with his son. It wasn't long before I could see

50

that this guy had issues with women. Issues he needed to work through without me putting myself in a position to bear the brunt of his frustrations.

3. He does not have a steady job or career goals: Now, I know this is going to ruffle a lot of feathers because as independent women, we have taken this nurturing thing with men to a whole new level. But if a man is broke, he has no business dating; especially not you! Men are supposed to be the protector and providers for their families. If he cannot pay his own bills and govern his financial affairs, then he is definitely not ready to provide for you or a family. Stop falling in love with a man's potential so you can clearly see his reality. Girl, toss that lemon back and run!

4. He does not respect your values or spiritual beliefs: For some reason, we just love ourselves some bad boys. It seems like the worse they are for us, the more we gravitate to them thinking that we can somehow change them. It's ok not to all say amen at once! My sister, if you are dating a man and the longer you are around him, the more you find yourself compromising your values, standards, or spiritual beliefs, then you are dealing with a lemon. Throw him back. A man who wants to be with you will respect those things about you that he doesn't understand. Now, I'm not insinuating that the man God has for you is perfect. When my mother married my father, he was a chain smoker and went to church on special occasions. But my father had respect for my mother's beliefs and values. He eventually came into his own sense of spirituality, quit smoking, and served faithfully in the church until the day he went home to be with the Lord. So change is possible. But respect for your values and spiritual beliefs is non-negotiable.

The major point that I want you to take away from this chapter is that you are worth the wait. I'm not talking about waiting to have sex. What I am saying is that you are worth the process. Don't cheapen yourself by latching hold to the first man who comes along and pays you some attention or compliments you. Don't be flattered that he wants to sit around with you all day and spend every waking moment together when he should be out working to provide for his future family.

Raise your standards ladies. Learn to not only be intentional in your dating but selective in who you spend your time with. When you go to the produce section do you just pick up a few pieces of fruit, throw them in the bag, and move on to the next aisle? No, you examine your fruit selections to make sure you are choosing the best in the bunch. So if you can do that with your fruit, then why wouldn't you do that with the men you choose to date?

If you have not identified what your standards and chore values are, then you have work to do. Purchase a journal and begin to write down your thoughts, dreams, and ambitions. Also, identify those things that you want in a mate that are non-negotiable. I'm not referring to a six figure salary or a Mercedes S-Class vehicle. I'm talking about the intangible things that you need in a mate that money can't buy like integrity, respect, faithfulness, and a strong sense of family. You can't know what you need from him until you actually identify what is important to you. What are your chore values? What are your spiritual beliefs? Once you know who you are and what you value in a mate, it makes it that much easier to identify the lemons and quickly throw them back.

66 *For by wise counsel you can wage your war, and in an abundance of counselors there is victory and safety.* *99*

Proverbs 24:6

10

Preparation For The Promise

One of the biggest challenges that I have faced in life is the ability to forgive. People, especially church folks, will tell you that it's easy. That is the furthest thing from the truth. However, without forgiveness, there is no growth. Without growth there is no maturity and a lack of maturity will hinder you from walking into your destiny.

Forgiveness is one of those foundational principles in life that must be in place before a new structure can be built. Who is it that you're holding on to? What do you want that you have not received yet? What have you lost that was so devastating that you stopped believing and trusting in God? What negative event in your life is holding you hostage to the nothingness of un-forgiveness? What is the thing that follows you like a dark cloud in the sky before the rain?

For me, it was the void of companionship. At one point in my life every man I loved, I eventually lost. I could pretty much time it to the day when things would start to fall apart. Either there was a previous relationship with ties that had not been severed, they lost interest, or I found myself in competition with another man or woman for their affections. With every negative situation, I grew colder and less enthused about love, relationships, and marriage. I started to believe that happiness in this area was just not for me. As I watched everyone else find the love of their life and float off into the future together on a cloud of pure bliss, I became more frustrated and aggravated with my own circumstances. I drew further and further away from God. I felt betrayed because I had given The Lord my life. I served in the church, gave my tithes, and helped other people establish healthy relationships. But the one thing I longed for, I still did not have. I wanted to know why. Why me? I was empty inside but wore the smile I was expected to wear on the outside. I was hurting while healing others.

Then I began to think, was I really ready for the love of my life to come and a family to follow? I was working two jobs with varying schedules. When would I actually have time to be courted? I had things on my credit that needed to be fixed, weight that needed to be lost, and the list goes on and on. I discovered that if I wanted God's best, I needed to strive to be at my best first! I didn't need to have it all together, but for the caliber of man that I was believing God for, looks alone wouldn't cut it. So, I gathered my school supplies, created a vision board, and went to work on me. There was something about seeing those images every day when I woke up that compelled me to want to do and be better.

I also realized that I had to open myself up to the possibilities of a healthy relationship and stop planting the same seeds if I wanted to reap a different harvest. That revelation in itself was an eyeful! It was not about the waiting process at all. It was about my inability to buckle down and get prepared for the life I wanted to have. Why would God send me the man of my dreams if I was out of shape with bad credit and baggage? Surely He wants just as much for His son as He wants for me, His daughter. So the next key to waiting is preparation. The more serious you become about your preparation process, the shorter the time will be to get to the promise.

Your body is a temple. And your appearance is the first impression that you will have on a potential mate. So get in the gym and work it out! Comb your hair. Take that fast food money, put it in a jar and save up for some new clothes. Basic, classic wardrobe pieces go a long way. Invest in your personal development. Stop allowing work, the grocery store, church, and home to be the only places you go. Step out of your comfort zone and go to a party, make plans to attend a festival or conference with your girlfriends, go paint balling, skiing, or horseback riding. Do something to break out of the ordinary! Life is bigger than the next thing you want God to do. There's a whole world out there with people in it who desire to have a companion like you. Stop waiting and start preparing. Do your part and I promise you, God will do His!

Just as there is a gravitational pull in the natural that brings you back down to earth when you jump, there is a gravitational pull that happens in the spirit realm as well. Un-forgiveness is one of the strongest weapons that the enemy will use to hold you back. While you spend your days constantly reliving what happened to you, the other person has gone on and is living their life. Some of the greatest apologies you will ever get are the ones that you will never hear. When we learn to release those people who have hurt us, we truly learn how to live. Even if you never talk to or see that person who hurt you again, when you say out of your mouth, "I forgive you" and become determined to walk in that forgiveness, the gravitational pull of un-forgiveness has to relinquish its hold on your destiny. I can't stress this enough. Learn to forgive! Not for the sake of the other person, but for the fate of your destiny!

Now you may ask, how do I forgive after struggling with this hurt for so long? The first step is acknowledging that the hurt exists. I will go back to a point I raised before. Keep a journal. Writing is one of the most therapeutic gifts that you can give yourself. It is an excellent way to cleanse the soul and give yourself a voice on your journey to forgiveness. The second step, seek professional help. I am an advocate for counseling and receiving psychological support from a licensed therapist. Receiving a graduate degree in psychology has opened up another level of compassion and advocacy in me for helping people get the clinical attention they need to overcome life's traumatic experiences. I know this statement is going to cause a great deal of controversy, but I'm going to say it anyway because I want you to be free. Everything can't be prayed away. If your goal is to live your best life now, then understand that there is no shame in seeking professional help to get there.

My third and final point on the process to forgiveness is do not go back to the thing that hurt you. The person who abused you may be dead and gone, but the spirit of that person can still manifest in other people. Have you ever wondered why you are attracted to the same type of guy? Or why you find yourself in the same compromising situation over and over again? It's because you are attracted to a particular spirit. It is familiar to you so you gravitate to it. One of the greatest tricks of the enemy to keep you away from your destiny is distraction. When he can no longer get you to lie, cheat, or abuse substances, he has to take his tactics to the next level. As long as your attention is on everything else except what God has called you to do, distraction will continue to rule in your life. Please remember the enemy's sole purpose is to steal, kill, and destroy your destiny by any means necessary. So resistance to his plan is futile.

When you release someone from your life, the struggle is not about going back to that person. You can successfully move on from them. I need you to elevate your thinking and understand this. The fight becomes about resisting the gravitational pull of the negative spirit that tries to lure you back into behaviors that you have been delivered from. Trust and believe if you have overcome it, temptation is coming to test your deliverance. But here is the good news, you are stronger and wiser than any distraction from the enemy. Walk confidently in your deliverance. You have the keys to prepare for the promise through the freedom of forgiveness.

> *But for right now, until that completeness, we have three things to do to lead us toward that consummation: Trust steadily in God, hope unswervingly, love extravagantly. And the best of the three is love.*

1 Corinthians 13:13

11

The Truth About Love

When it comes to relationships, we often look for the whirlwind romance. The butterflies that tickle your stomach, the heart racing with anticipation whenever he is near, and the undeniable chemistry you feel as your bodies connect at the height of passion. But you must ask yourself, do any of these things have substance? Can chemistry hold us together when everything is falling apart? Are those butterfly wings strong enough to cover us when life starts to hit from every angle?

So what is love? Is it a feeling or is it fortitude? Is it the security of knowing that you are surrounded and covered or is it the words and schematics that make you feel good? Just to name a few of its attributes, love is patient, kind, unconditional, and holds no record of wrong. Now ask yourself, do these elements exist within my relationship? Does it hold its shape like a diamond, or is it as volatile as a cloud of glitter? Love is more than a feeling. Love is resilient. No matter how many heartbreaks we endure, we still believe in it. Love is durable. Like a precious stone that holds its shine, love remains through the test of time.

It's amazing how we can have this grandiose vision of our ideal soul mate. Many of us, when asked, can give you a full description down to their hair texture, eye color, and physical build of what we want in a man. We can tell you what kind of car we want him to drive, home we want him to live in and career we desire for him to have. But most of us never marry our ideal mate. We end up with someone so far left of what we imagined. This is for good reason.

If you aspire to be married, there are fundamental, basic essentials that he needs to possess. Does he respect your values and spiritual beliefs? Has he seen you at your worst and still said you were beautiful...and meant it? If you have children, can you trust him to be a good provider and father figure? Is he courteous and gracious to you in public and to your family and friends? Is he loyal, trustworthy, and a good steward over his finances? That list doesn't sound very romantic does it? I didn't think so. When the Bible describes love, it never says love is fine as wine with a nice behind. Nor does it say his voice is so smooth, he can sell ice to an Eskimo.

In 1 Corinthians 13:4-7 (AMP), the Apostle Paul provides a very distinct description of what love is. Let's take a moment to break his description down and apply it to our outlook on love and relationships.

"Love endures long and is patient and kind; love never is envious nor boils over with jealousy, is not boastful or vainglorious, does not display itself haughtily."

Ladies, if you find yourself constantly dimming your light so he can shine brighter, that is not love. The man that God has for you should support you in all of your endeavors. He should be your number one cheerleader and biggest fan.

"[Love] is not conceited (arrogant and inflated with pride); it is not rude (unmannerly) and does not act unbecomingly. Love (God's love in us) does not insist on its own rights or its own way, for it is not self-seeking; it is not touchy or fretful or resentful; it takes no account of the evil done to it [it pays no attention to a suffered wrong]."

Apostle Paul touches on a very important point here. Love is about compromise, give and take, and sometimes learning to agree to disagree. If you are dating a man who does not value your opinion or doesn't respect the fact that you have one at all, that's not love. If he finds every opportunity to degrade you or make you feel inadequate in public and private, that's not love. A woman who thinks for herself and has an opinion is priceless. Never allow someone to diminish the things about you that make you great. "[Love] does not rejoice at injustice and unrighteousness, but rejoices when right and truth prevail. Love bears up under anything and everything that comes, is ever ready to believe the best of every person, its hopes are fadeless under all circumstances, and it endures everything [without weakening]."

Love is strength. When a person is loved properly, they grow stronger spiritually. Love sustains and adds value to your life. If every time you and your partner have a disagreement, he leaves for days instead of sticking it out until you all reach a resolve, that's not love. There is a stick and stay power in true love that is unmatched. I know none of this sounds whimsical or romantic. But this is the truth about love. Although Paul's account is not the totality of all that love is, this passage is a great point of reference. Yes, a tall, well built, handsome man would be ideal. But if he does not possess the fundamental traits of love, you are setting yourself up for years of heartache and un-fulfillment.

I remember when my best friend was ready to take the bold step towards marriage and she had two suitors. There was the one that had the outward presentation all together. He was a youth Pastor, charismatic, a sharp dresser, handsome, and definitely knew his way around the English language. The brother was smooth. Then there was the other guy. He was quiet, reserved, kind, an avid student of the Word, and hard working. Needless to say, he didn't give my friend goose bumps or butterflies. In fact, she had turned down his advances on so many occasions, I wondered why the poor guy hadn't given up. One day in conversation, after seeing that she was visibly perplexed about this life-changing decision, I took a sheet of paper, wrote both of the gentleman's names at the top, and drew a line down the middle. I asked her to list all of their good qualities. By the time she finished this exercise, she had to use the back side of the paper to finish the list of positive qualities for guy number two. She passed the paper back to me, I looked at it, and slid it back across the table to her. Then I said with a smile, "I think you have your answer." My best friend and "the other guy" were married a year later. They have moved into a beautiful home, travel regularly, they are financially stable as a team, and have given birth to their first child.

The moral of the story is, don't get caught up in the one who sweeps you off your feet. Get swept away by the one who can help you stay on your feet during life's most turbulent times. For women, love equals security. So your mate should be a firm foundation upon which love can grow. A man can be average to most, but if he has the ability to keep your love tank full, he will be Superman to you. Wisdom dictates that we focus on the fundamentals of love and not the frills of emotions. Emotions are fleeting, but real love is forever.

" Be completely humble and gentle; be patient, bearing with one another in love. "

Ephesians 4:2

12

Love Is An Action Word

One of the worst things you can do to yourself in a relationship is try to convince someone of your worth. Have you ever thought that maybe it's not meant for them to see who you really are? Our Father does all things well. There are times His love will shield us from what we want, so He can get us to what we deserve.

So why are you going through the motions trying to get him to see who you really are when God has placed blinders over his eyes to protect you? As a single woman, your job is to enjoy your journey. When the Master is done molding you, the man that He has for you will be there to celebrate everything about you that the others were too blind to see.

Maybe you feel like your time will never come because God is taking so long to send your knight in shining armor. First of all, he is not a knight. He won't be your savior. His job is not to make you whole or complete. Why would God send someone into your life to take His place? But what he will be is a protector and provider. He will be the one that is equipped to stand with you through the trials and triumphs of life. He will be a man after God's own heart.

My sister, don't be blinded by the world's concept of love. Be a woman that seeks the Word of God to know what love really is. Practice the love of Christ in your everyday relationships. Don't just preserve your love for when the one comes along. Love is an action word and is meant to be shared freely like the air we breathe. It is not to be preserved for a select few or an audience of one. Your love is to be expressed daily so those that experience it will be strengthened.

Remember it was Ruth's love for Naomi that won the heart of Boaz. She wasn't in the field gleaning for herself. She was enduring the backbreaking field work so she could provide for the mother of her deceased husband. Now that's love. She could have easily given in to Naomi's pleas for her and Orpah to return to Moab. But she chose to be obedient to God and to love Naomi as she would her own mother. This won her the hand of one of the wealthiest land owners in the region.

Here's another key to the waiting process. Don't concern yourself with the one who rejected you, because God is speaking your name to the one who is made for you. Love with the intention to bless someone else; not for self-gratification or gain. The one that God designed for you is watching. He is observing your accomplishments. He is even watching what you post on social media. He may even be that familiar face at Starbucks who is observing how you treat the cashier when they get your order wrong. Take every opportunity to love with your whole heart. The love you show to others will bring you one step closer to the one who will love you for a lifetime.

And I will restore or replace for you the years that the locust has eaten—the hopping locust, the stripping locust, and the crawling locust, My great army which I sent among you.

Joel 2:25

13

Why Do We Stay After The Love Is Gone?

Many of the negative behaviors that we display in our relationships were cultivated during our formative years and only become stronger as we get older. As I became older, I realized a very powerful thing about myself. I don't let go easily. Growing up, I experienced a great deal of fighting in the home. My parents disagreed on everything from money to whether or not my hair should be hot combed. Needless to say, the internalization of these battles left me traumatized and I was diagnosed with an anxiety disorder at a very young age. When I started to form my own relationships, I developed a pattern of becoming a people pleaser. If I felt that I was losing the person, I would try harder and do more to stay in their good graces and ultimately convince them to stay with me. I would become nervous, anxious, and consumed with the task of winning them over. These behaviors left me depressed because instead of realizing that God was turning the page in the relationship for my good, I took it as though I was doing something wrong.

Most relationships in life have an expiration date. If you stay past your time, things will turn sour and ultimately your heart will grow cold. But even though we know the inevitable is going to happen, the heart still wants to hold on after the mind knows it's time to move on. So the inner battle begins. By the time you accept the fact that the relationship is over, you are left with the realization that you've wasted valuable, precious time trying to breathe life into a dead situation. But here's what I love about God. Even after we are too stubborn to realize that the break-up is for our good, His Word says He will still redeem the time.

That is the kind of merciful and loving God we serve. I have always said that self-examination is good for the soul. But when it comes to the heart doing what the head knows is right, now that's a different story. In these times, you must ask God to give you the strength to move on and the patience to actively wait for the person that He has for you. You don't have to try to do it alone. Let the one who made you, help you. It may be uncomfortable for a while. But just as a mother endures pain during the birth of her child, pain is necessary to birth you into your place of purpose.

I saw an illustration of a young girl holding on to a small teddy bear and God kneeling down asking her to give the bear to Him. Behind His back, He was holding a larger teddy bear that He planned to give to the little girl in place of the small one that she was tightly holding on to. This is what happens when we hold on to relationships that are past their expiration date. God is asking you to give Him the thing you are holding captive in exchange for the better thing that He has for you. Understand that God is Alpha and Omega. He is the God of a finished work. Trust Him with your end and your beginning because He made you. He wrote your life story before He gave you life.

Letting go is never easy and in some instances, it takes time. Never allow anyone to dictate the timeframe of your healing process. That is between you and God. The first step is to give the situation to Him and resist the urge to go back and pick it up. He already carried that burden to the cross for you. Although the pain is necessary, the promise is guaranteed. Let Him give you beauty for ashes and replace joy where there was once pain.

Letting go of a failed relationship can be challenging for so many reasons. One of the biggest excuses that I hear all the time is staying together for the children. I am the product of two parents who tried to stay together for over seventeen years for the children and they made our lives a nightmare in the process. In fact, my parents were better apart than they ever were together. Now before the moral police write my citation, let me say this. I am in no way advocating divorce. I believe that couples should do everything they can to bring healing and restoration to their relationship. But once you have done all you can, and it's still not working, it's time to let go.

Another excuse that we tell ourselves is no one will want me. This trick of the enemy is the furthest thing from the truth. I have countless friends and family members who moved on after a divorce and are now in successful, fulfilling second marriages. My sister, it can be done. You have the strength to let go of what no longer serves you. You have the strength to believe for a better, greater, stronger love than you could ever imagine.

Many of us put our faith in a man more than God. When the relationship has run its course and it's time to turn the page, we say things like, "what am I going to do without him?" I have a three word answer to that question. YOU WILL LIVE! Just like the little girl in the illustration who was holding on to the teddy bear, you have to let go of the life you built for yourself so God can give you His abundant life. I'm not telling you something that I heard. This is what I know. As long as the enemy can keep you distracted with mediocrity, you will never experience extraordinary.

66 *You who have made me see many troubles and calamities will revive me again; from the depths of the earth you will bring me up again. You will increase my greatness and comfort me again.* 99

Psalms 71:20-21

14

If It Don't Fit, Leave It

I have always had serious detachment issues; whether it's in relationships, friendships, or just changing jobs. It is always a daunting task for me to turn the page so a new chapter can begin. When my parents would fight, my mother would pack us up and leave the house. There were numerous times when we would stay with my aunt for a few days or a week until things blew over. I remember countless times that I would stand between my parents or grab on to my father's leg in hopes that my presence would make the arguing stop. But it never worked. I had become invisible in this situation.

As a little girl, my father would shower me with gifts. We would go everywhere together. I was his little shadow. My father would throw me in the air and as I fell into his arms, he would tell me how much he loved me. Then one day, all the love and attention just stopped. No more beautiful dresses, no more shadowing, no more throwing me in the air and falling into his arms. It just stopped. I felt abandoned; as if my father had turned his back on me. Sure I was older now and was becoming a young lady. But at the time I needed my father's affirmation, compliments, and guidance the most, he was not there for me.

As a young adult, I carried these separation issues into my relationships. I lived with the desire to always try to make things right. The more a man resisted, the harder I would try. I developed a pattern of choosing relationships that kept me striving for perfection in the eyes of a man that I would never reach. I continued to try to make them fit to the point where I accepted mental and physical abuse. To the world I portrayed a strong, independent woman. But inside, I was still that broken little girl longing for her father's acceptance. I knew I couldn't continue to live this way. The lack of fulfillment had become unbearable. So, I decided to turn to the one who knew me best. God began to take me back to the root cause of the patterns and compelled me to face the pain of my father's rejection. It is by the grace of God that I am now an overcomer. Because of Him, I now know that I am enough.

My sister, you do not have to force acceptance. In order to be whole, you must know within yourself that you are enough. You are good enough. You are pretty enough. You are smart enough. You are bold enough to walk in victory. You no longer have to live under a cloud of shame from abuse, rejection, and pain. When we try to force relationships to work, it's like taking two random puzzle pieces and using everything we have to put them together.

Too many of us are in what I call "if I could just" relationships. If I could just get him to go to church, he will change. If I could just get him to see the real me, he would love me. If I could just have his baby, he will see what a good wife and mother I can be. Stop the madness! Whatever you do to win him, you will have to do twice as much to keep him. Now do you really want to live the rest of your life under that kind of pressure? I hope the answer is no.

When God put Adam in a deep sleep and made Eve, he woke up and his vision for her was clear. He knew who she was because she was designed just for him. So take courage and find solace in the fact that no matter what the statistics say, God has someone for you that he designed before the foundation of the earth. No statistic, shortage, or time clock can change that. God wants to give you sweat- less victories in every area of your life; relationships included. Anything that is forced will eventually fall apart. Allow God to bring your relationships together organically in His time and due season. If it doesn't fit, then you have the strength my sister to leave it.

" But I have raised you up for this very purpose, that I might show you my power and that my name might be proclaimed in all the earth. "

Exodus 9:16

15

Settling Leads To Struggling

There are times when the wait for God's best can become so intense that you start to get anxious. The thought creeps into your mind that maybe God needs a little help or a gentle nudge in the relationship department. So you go out seeking for companionship in clubs, on social media, and even at church. The enemy is aware of the anxiety that is ensuing so he brings suitors your way. The type that I like to call "Mr. Almost Right". You know, full of potential but just haven't quite turned the corner to receive the manifestation yet. The ones that will say all the things you want to hear and do just enough to keep you hanging on.

So you start to date Mr. Almost Right and although the red flags are flying everywhere, you're already convinced that you can "fix" him. Or in time, once he sees how awesome of a woman you are, he will want to be and do better. This is called settling; and settling ultimately leads to struggling. Whether it's providing financial support for him or a lack of emotional stability and support for you, the longer you settle the more real the struggle becomes. A deficiency starts to form which causes a breach in your happiness, confidence, and even your spiritual connection with God. Sound familiar? We all have been guilty of this. Settling for an underdeveloped man because you can't bear the anxiety of waiting on God any longer. Struggling emotionally, physically, and financially to hold on to someone that God never meant for you, is a dead end situation. Yes, the relationship may get you more likes on Facebook or a few nods of approval from family members. But have you ever thought about how much you are losing in the process? And if you will be honest with yourself, the sacrifice of your time, emotional stability and finances is far greater than anything this man is providing. Some of us have been there; while others of us are still there.

Today's society has perverted the gender roles in the family structure. It has become the norm for women to be the provider for the family. When you settle for a man who is immature or underdeveloped, you accept a weight of responsibility that you were never meant to carry. It's also very difficult for those who love you to sympathize with your frustrations because accepting this role was ultimately your choice. If the man that you are taking care of is the father of your children, he still does not get a pass. There are many women who feel just as lonely with a man sleeping right next to them every night as a single woman with no prospects. My sister, having a man is not what completes you. It is the fulfillment of walking in your purpose that does.

At the core of settling lies the desire for companionship. This is a very real, human emotion that can be both a blessing and a curse. If God said that it is not good for man to be alone, then what do we do with these feelings of loneliness? Do we suppress them and put on a fake smile like we are happy? Do we come home from work every day, close the curtains, pull the covers up to our chin and cry ourselves to sleep? So what is one to do while you are waiting? The key to overcoming loneliness is to make an impact. Purpose has a way of giving you a sense of belonging and wholeness. When you discover your purpose, you are on the right path to making an impact that will fill the void of loneliness.

" I know that You can do all things, And that no thought or purpose of Yours can be restrained. "

Job 42:2

16

How Do I Make An Impact?

If you are struggling with loneliness and un-fulfillment, my advice to you is to discover your purpose. Invest in it with your time and talents so intensely, that by the time you lay your head down at night all you can do is sleep. Be so intentional in your purpose that there is no time to be anxious about when God will send your future husband. Identifying your purpose is not rocket science. It is simply the thing that you would get up to do every day without a paycheck. It is your passion. It is the thing that excites you so much that when you talk about it, there is a fire in your eyes that is undeniable. It is like air to you. It is the quintessential essence of who you are. It is the very thing that will put you in position for the man that God has for you to find you.

Boaz found Ruth out in the fields gleaning. She was intentionally working to fulfill her promise to Naomi. Providing for her widowed mother in law became her purpose. Your purpose does not have to be something extravagant and world changing. You just have to discover what it is and walk in it. The man that God has for you is not going to randomly knock on your door one day, get down on one knee in your living room, and profess his love for you. It is left up to you to get up, get out, and do something meaningful so the universe can apply the positive energy that you are giving off to the law of attraction.

So ask yourself, what is the one thing you can do that makes you happy? My sister that is your purpose. For some it may be artistic for others it may be civic or political in nature, and for someone else it may be humanitarian. But whatever your purpose is, it is uniquely designed for you and someone in this world needs what you have to offer. Someone needs the deposit that you are destined to make in the earth to in turn discover their purpose. Nothing that happens in our lives is for us. Our experiences set the stage for the evolution of humanity. You have been placed on this earth to make a difference. I challenge you to discover what your purpose is and carry it through!

66 Therefore, since we are surrounded by so great a cloud of witnesses [who by faith have testified to the truth of God's absolute faithfulness], stripping off every unnecessary weight and the sin which so easily and cleverly entangles us, let us run with endurance and active persistence the race that is set before us. 99

Hebrews 12:1

17

Push Through It

Giving birth to your purpose can be one of the scariest yet exhilarating experiences of your life. With any birth, there is always pain. But I encourage you my sister to push through it. You were created to bear the pain of the birthing process and emerge victorious. However, on your journey to purpose there will always be obstacles. Now let's talk about some of the obstacles that can impede the birthing process.

1. Self- esteem: You can be your own worst enemy when it comes to walking in your purpose. When you become bold enough to step out of the boat of mediocrity, the enemy will try to resurrect every negative thing about you in an attempt to make you sink. But just as Jesus called

Peter out of the boat and commanded that he walk on water, He is calling you to do what to some would seem impossible. My sister, it does not matter who you used to be. All that matters is who you are becoming. God doesn't wait until we have reached perfection to use us. If that were the case, none of us would have a chance. In our weakness, His strength is made perfect and that is all the perfection we need.

2. Finances: If what God has called you to do does not exceed what you can do for yourself, then you are not thinking big enough. When God gives you the vision, He has already established the provision. It is up to us to be in the right place at the right time to receive it. I'll never forget when God gave me the vision for IMAGE Magazine in 1999. I had no idea where I would get the resources to pull off such a huge project. But I wrote the vision down in a proposal and made it plain. Five years later, God used an unassuming gentleman, who happened to have major influence with the city, to bless me with a grant that not only helped me start the magazine, but kept us financially sound for the first five years that we were in business. I am a witness that there is nothing too hard for God. If he gives you a vision, your only job is to be obedient and patient enough for the provision to manifest.

3. Family: Now let's talk about the blessing and curse that we call family. Family is a blessing because they have been there all of your life. But they can be a curse because they also know your past. Either way, family can be a definite obstacle when it comes to pushing through to your purpose. Purpose is a birthing process. The closer you get to the time of delivery, the smaller the number of people allowed in the birthing room becomes. Everyone in your family can not handle your vision. When Joseph told his brothers that one day he would be king and that they would bow to him, they threw him in a ditch and sold him into slavery. So be careful who you articulate your vision to because everyone won't be happy for you.

No matter what obstacle you face on your journey to destiny, push through it. Make a commitment to yourself and God to see what is on the other side of that dream that you have held in your heart for so many years. Keep your mind open to the possibilities. I am a living witness that the manifestation of destiny is possible. How do I know? Because you are reading this book.

" But as for you, be strong and do not lose courage, for there is reward for your work. "

2 Chronicles 15:7

18

Goal Diggers And People Builders

I am a people builder in the purest form. Which means, if a person stays around me for a significant amount of time, their life is going to change for the better. It may be something as monumental as finding their life's purpose; to something as simple as upgrading their style. Even though this gift comes naturally to me, I discovered that my people building skills were not always embraced by the men in my life. Or, they may have been accepting of me building them up and supporting their dreams at first, but when commitment and accountability came into play, most of them chose to exit stage left.

Then one day I had an "aha moment". I was expecting more from the men in my life than they had the capacity to give. Even though I wanted better for them, they ultimately had to want better for themselves. As women, we believe that we can change a man's level of ambition by loving him to better. But you can't and you won't. Sure, they may step their game up in the beginning to impress you. But if the ambition to achieve more in life is not in their heart, they will eventually settle for something or someone that matches who and where they really are.

Another bitter truth to being a people builder is that the other party will take advantage of your gift, but disregard you in the process. Here's an example of what I mean. Has a guy you were dating ever asked you for style advice? You accept the challenge and go all out to make sure his outfit is on point. You all arrive at the party together but you watch him soak up compliments and flirt with every woman in the room while barely acknowledging your existence. Not a good feeling, is it?

My sister, don't cheapen your gift. People building and goal digging should be reserved for the one who is actively making an investment in you. So often, we make the mistake of dropping our whole life to support a man's dreams. But if he is not married or engaged to you, that's not your job. Yes, I know it's tight. But it's right! You see, when Ruth was discovered by Boaz, she was handling her business. She was taking care of the needs of her household. I am not saying don't support him at all. But make sure his effort matches your worth first. I encourage you to follow the law of reciprocity when using these gifts. Give what you get in return. I know you may think this sounds selfish, but in the end, when you are able to leave the relationship with your self-worth intact and your head held high, you will thank me.

Spiritualist Iyanla Vanzant once said, "when we give too much of ourselves to someone, we unknowingly make the other person a thief." There is so much truth to this statement because when we give to others what we need for our soul's survival, we deplete our reserves which ultimately leaves us empty and unfulfilled. Your singleness is your time to be selfish. It is your opportunity to focus on the greatness that's within you. Many of us are frustrated because we cast the net of our time, love, attention, and virtue in the wrong pond. We self-sabotage our own happiness because we make decisions based on our ideals of what love should be. When all we have to do is get before the Lord, find out what our life's purpose is and ask for His guidance on how we are to carry it through. I can't stress this enough, it is your purpose not people that positions you for greatness.

A good woman is hard to find, and worth far more than diamonds. Her husband trusts her without reserve, and never has reason to regret it. Never spiteful, she treats him generously all her life long.

Proverbs 31:10-12

19

Paying The Cost To Be The Boss

One of the hardest lessons I learned as an ambitious single woman is that you will pay a price for being driven. Ladies, taking a step back to stand in a man's shadow never works. If you try it, you may be able to fool yourself for a while, but eventually you will lose yourself and become bitter and resentful of the decision you made to compromise. There is a difference between submitting your vision under the covering of your spouse and forfeiting it all together to support his vision. When you make the decision to be all that God has created you to be, to an insecure man, it can be threatening. Now I am in no way telling you to go around flaunting or bragging about your accomplishments. If you are genuine and gracious in your countenance, your virtuous qualities will speak for themselves. Your gifts will always make room for you and place you before great men. One of those great men could very well be your husband.

A man who is confident in who he is will always want his woman to shine. He will enhance her light and not overcast her virtue with his insecurities. He will speak well of her and praise her accomplishments every chance he gets. When a man is proud of you, he is your greatest ally. If he is jealous of you, he can become your worst enemy. Sleeping with the enemy is real and can be detrimental. So when you allow a man to pursue you, be sure that he is interested in you and not the benefits that come along with keeping you around.

The more accomplished you become, the smaller the pool of men you have to choose from will be. Although the pool gets smaller, there are still men out there who appreciate a goal oriented woman. There are men who are willing and ready to match your worth. So do not compromise. Society may demonize women who refuse to lower their standards. But you are a precious jewel and your value is priceless. Having standards never goes out of style. You are worth the wait. I'll say it again, YOU ARE WORTH THE WAIT!! God is in control of your destiny and your love story has already been written.

" Nevertheless neither is the man without the woman, neither the woman without the man, in the Lord. "

1 Corinthians 11:11

20

The Untaught Need

One day while scrolling through my timeline on Facebook I saw a meme that really shook me. It read, "White/ Hispanic women are taught how to keep a man while Black women are taught how to live without one." I pondered on this statement for a minute and couldn't understand why I was personally bothered by its message. Then I began to reflect on how I was raised to think about men and relationships. I also began to think back on conversations I have had with Black women about men and the many disappointments they have faced surrounding relationships. Many of my friends are single mothers who have been abandoned and let down by the fathers of their children. Some of my friends, including myself, have experienced unproductive relationships and as a result have never been married and do not have children.

Regardless of the circumstances, we all have one thing in common. We have mastered the art of survival. We have learned how to provide for and protect ourselves in the absence of men who have not accepted their roles in our lives. For many of us, it goes back to our fathers not being there. Or in my case, having a father who was in the home physically, but provided little to no parental and spiritual guidance.

In most cases, like mine and countless others, the mother picks up the slack. She steps into survival mode to keep the home moving as it should. So she becomes the protector and provider not out of desire but out of necessity. Being the product of a "surviving" Black woman, I watched my mother make sacrifices and decisions that she should have never been left to make on her own. As a result, she raised her sons to be good men in spite of my father's shortcomings and raised her daughters to be independent women because we too may have to live with a lack of male presence one day. This train of thought yielded very different outcomes. My brothers have become superheroes to their families, while my sister and I have mastered being single super women.

Although I commend my mother for raising me to get an education, make my own money, and go after the things I want in life, I realized that I have been taught to survive and not thrive in relationships with the opposite sex. I, like many other women, was taught the unwritten rule that you do what you have to do for yourself just in case he never does. But I had to ask myself, what have you given up to gain independence? The answer is simple, my vulnerability. I have asked several men who are close to me why they think I am still single and in so many words they have told me it is because I act like I don't need a man. And of course my reply would always be, how is that so? I'm single and want to be married with a family. Surely I need a man for that, right?

Although many of my male friends had great responses, once I began to search within myself for the answer to this misunderstood piece of my character, I discovered a key component of my femininity that makes me attractive to men is my ability to be vulnerable. I had to face the harsh reality that I wasn't open to allowing a man to make a deposit in my life. And the ability to make a healthy, positive deposit in the life of the woman he loves is how a man knows that he is needed. I realized that although I have a lot to contribute to the needs in his life, he also has a lot and in some areas more to contribute to the needs in mine. The ability to be vulnerable with each other and allow ourselves to be each other's strength is what forms an undeniable bond. In essence, learning to cope with the absence of love does not replace the lack of and need for love.

When you truly desire companionship, you must first look at yourself and take ownership of the mindsets, attitudes and behaviors that you have allowed to govern your outlook on love and relationships. Many of us have had to live in survival mode to maintain our household's familial structure due to the absence of a strong, affirming male presence. For so long we have watched our mothers hold down multiple jobs, overcome abuse, infidelity and many other insurmountable obstacles in relationships, that it becomes a daily struggle to keep history from repeating itself. But in all that we have experienced, in all that our eyes have seen and our hearts have endured, we must learn not to lose our sensitivity. We must learn to maintain our vulnerability in spite of our reality. Your vulnerability is not worthy of being exposed to just any man, though. He must first be vetted and you must be sure that he is the man you are comfortable opening up to. Exposing your vulnerabilities to the wrong person can prove detrimental.

So how do I learn to need you, when I have been taught to live without you? How do I let you in, when I've been taught to push you away? Just be, my sister. Be free to let your feelings and emotions flow. Stop trying to hold it all together emotionally for everyone else and give yourself room to feel, to breathe, to need, to grieve, and to grow. Allow the man that comes into your life to see all of you. If you feel like crying in front of him, cry. If you need twenty dollars until pay day, ask. If the light bulb is blown, let him fix it. Men are protectors and providers by nature. The more you open yourself up to receive, the more he will provide. The more you open yourself up to be emotionally vulnerable, the more he will desire to protect you.

Yes, we have all had our hearts broken several times. But the good news is, your sensitivity does not have to be lost in the healing process. Ask God to send the man into your life that has the ability to compliment you physically, spiritually, emotionally, and mentally. The ultimate goal in any relationship is to compliment not complete each other. And when he comes, refrain from making him your pet project. See him as he was created to be, your protector and provider. He will not be a perfect man. But if you open yourself up to the possibilities, he will be the perfect man for you.

Give your entire attention to what God is doing right now, and don't get worked up about what may or may not happen tomorrow. God will help you deal with whatever hard things come up when the time comes.

Matthew 6:34

21

If Men Are Like Taxis, Then Why Can't I Catch One?

I was on a flight to Miami and had the opportunity to sit next to a young man who at first glance was very handsome, clean cut, and well built. When I finally got settled on board, we struck up a conversation and then I realized he was also articulate; which is a complete turn on for me. As we continued to talk, I learned that he was still enlisted in the Navy, worked as a flight attendant, and was in law school. A total package, right? Well, maybe. As the conversation progressed, my enthusiasm quickly dwindled. He revealed that he lived in Italy, was stationed out of New York, had a six year old daughter who lives in Chicago with her mother, and his parents lived in Boston. As I took a deep breath, I was forced to accept the fact that this handsome man was spread too thin. Although he was giving me all the signals, all I saw were the red flags.

As women, we believe that we are supposed to be the calm in the midst of the chaos in a man's life. When in all actuality, some men enjoy a chaotic lifestyle and will seek out a woman who only desires to go with the flow. If that does not work for you, and you prefer a more structured or routine lifestyle, then don't get involved with a man who has a lot going on. Men distinctly know where they are in life and if they are on a specific path to accomplish a goal, like this young man was, then the women that they meet and date along the way will only be seat fillers. Until a man truly accomplishes the goals that he has set for himself or at least gets to a point in his journey where he is temporarily satisfied, he will not be in a position to make you the star of his show. As I talked to this young man, I knew exactly where I would come up in this equation should I chose to get involved with him. Subsequently, I would be just another pawn on his chessboard. Because clearly he was not ready for a queen.

We often waste time getting intrigued by these types of situationships when we should have paid attention to the warning signs from the beginning, enjoyed the conversation, and kept it moving. Ladies, every man you meet, no matter how flirty or fine, is not husband material. Don't waste your time repeating the cycle of getting involved in relationships that are going nowhere. Men are like taxis. If their light is not on, you can run behind them, whistle loudly, wave wildly, and even stick out your perfectly shaped leg on the curve and he still won't stop to pick you up. When a man is ready for a committed relationship, he will incorporate you into his entire world; not just the parts that are convenient.

As the plane prepared to land, "Mr. Taxi" asked for my number. I graciously gave it to him, but I did not take his. I could tell my decline was a shock to him. But it also sent a clear signal that if he wanted to get to know me, he would have to make the first move. I had no desire to be the initiator. Many times when we come across a man who fits the description of our desired mate, we jump at the chance to be a part of his world. When in all actuality, we should do the exact opposite. Leave the ball in his court. If he is interested, he will pursue you.

" May he give you your heart's desire, and put all your purposes into effect. "

Psalm 20:4

CONCLUSION

It is my sincerest hope that this book has blessed you through reading it as much as it has blessed me through writing it. My one desire is for you to be free. That's what this whole journey is about. Embracing your emancipation from the bondage of when and stepping into the freedom of right now. I want you to believe in yourself and know that with God, all things are possible. But most importantly, always remember that waiting is an action word. Stop using waiting on God as an excuse and accept the fact that He is waiting on you. Love yourself enough to know that you are worth the wait; which is the process that we all must go through to walk in our greatness. Find your confidence in your purpose. Allow yourself to live your best life now and resist the temptation to put off those things that make you happy while you wait for your soulmate. Let him find you fulfilled, healthy, and whole with nothing missing and nothing broken.

I challenge you to dust off that journal and start writing the vision for your life as a single woman. Create a vision board so you can track your successes. Goals are merely dreams with deadlines. Reward yourself when you reach a goal and then set a new one. You have so much to offer this world. Never allow fear to stop you. I want to continue to walk with you on this journey. So please don't hesitate to send your emails to askfatima@fatimalhall.com or instant message me @FatimaLHall via social media. Let's celebrate our victories together and continue to evolve until we get there!

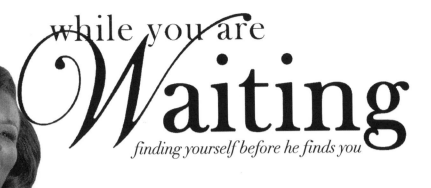

while you are Waiting

finding yourself before he finds you

CONNECT.
LIKE.
SHARE.

WE WANT TO HEAR FROM YOU!

JOIN THE CONVERSATION:

 @FatimaLHall

Visit the website:
www.**fatimalhall**.com

Fatima would love to come and share at your next event:
info@fatimalhall.com or 678.705.1680

81318394R00064

Made in the USA
San Bernardino, CA
06 July 2018